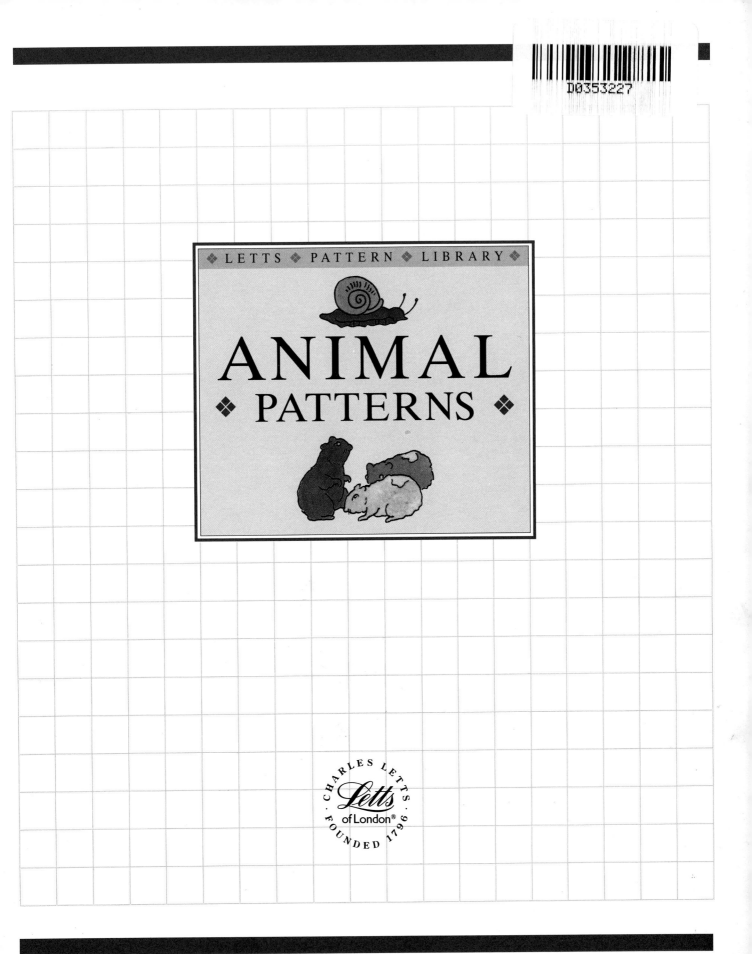

LETTS ✦ PATTERN ✦ LIBRARY

ANIMAL
PATTERNS

CHARLES LETTS
Letts
of London®
FOUNDED 1796

First published in 1992
by Charles Letts & Co Ltd
Letts of London House
Parkgate Road
London SW11 4NQ

Reprinted in 1992

Designed and edited by
Anness Publishing Ltd
Boundary Row Studios
1/7 Boundary Row
London SE1 8HP

Published in Australia in association with
J. B. Fairfax Press Pty Limited
by arrangement with
Charles Letts & Co Ltd
London, United Kingdom

© 1992 Charles Letts & Co Ltd

A CIP catalogue record for this book
is available from the British Library.

ISBN 1-85238-345-3

"Letts" is a registered trademark of
Charles Letts & Co Ltd.

Editorial Director: Joanna Lorenz
Art Director: Peter Bridgewater
Illustrator: Ivan Hissey

Printed and bound in Great Britain by
Butler & Tanner Ltd, Frome and London

CONTENTS

INTRODUCTION

The world of nature has been a source of wonder and inspiration to artists of every age, and animals have featured as themes and symbols in all kinds of decorative art and craft – from ancient and aboriginal cave paintings, to magnificent and noble embroidered heraldic devices, and on into the cartoon characters and comic strips of the modern generation. There are few craftspeople or hobbyists today – whether cake decorators, knitters, needle-workers, potters or painters – who do not constantly need to refer to and draw on images from the animal kingdom: thus *Animal Patterns* has been specially developed to provide a comprehensive visual dictionary of practical design possibilities and creative choices suitable for use in every craft medium.

The patterns in this book can be used in myriad ways. The following are just a few of the possible techniques and crafts for which they are suitable: stencilling, collage, block-printing, fabric painting, ceramic painting, painting onto wooden toys, crewel work, embroidery, appliqué work, watercolour and oil painting, cut-out work and so on. The patterns can be adapted for knitting or quilting, and they can also be used in sugarcraft, for buttercream and frosting designs, and novelty cakes.

With imagination, the basic patterns provided can be used to decorate a limitless variety of items – ornaments; cards, tags and gift-wraps; sweaters; cushion-covers; table-ware; friezes and hangings; pillows and bed-linen; toys, nursery furniture and many many others. They can be adapted for special occasions such as Christmas or Easter, or to customize a present for a favourite friend or relation. Don't be scared to experiment: mix and match among the various sections and images to create your own effects – in groups, such as a farmyard collage (or nativity scene) for a toddler, or in repeat patterns or motifs.

ADAPTING THE PATTERNS

The patterns have all been drawn in a very simple way, with no shading or fine inner line work, so that they are as easy as possible to use, and they allow the flexibility for you to add your own personal touches. You may decide to use them at various different sizes to fit a particular area of your work. Remember, too, that you can flip the patterns over using different techniques to give a mirror image of the design. Use your own creative skills and imagination when adapting these patterns.

The designs can be used individually, or a combination can be made into a tableau or repeat pattern. The easiest way to do this is to draw the chosen piece on tracing paper, then place the designs on top of each other and move them until you are happy with the arrangement. Finally, trace the whole thing and transfer it onto the required surface.

If you want to use the pattern at the same size you can simply trace the outline onto tracing paper, but if the design you want to use is too large or too small, you can enlarge or reduce it in two ways. One simple way is to use a photocopier with an enlarging and reducing mode, which will ensure that the design is faithfully reproduced; just copy the image to the size required. However, most machines only enlarge up to 156% of the original size, so you would have to use the machine twice if you wanted to double the size of the design. This method also depends of course on your having access to a photocopier with this facility, although an increasing number of shops now offer a photocopying service.

The other, traditional, method is to draw the image to a different size by hand, using the grid method. This is not difficult for most designs, although accuracy is important and you may have problems if the design is very intricate. The technique consists of drawing a grid of squares over the original design and then copying the design, square for square, onto a larger (or smaller, if you want to reduce the size) grid. In this book the designs are all drawn with ready-made grid lines, so that they can be transferred simply to another sheet of paper to an increased or reduced size.

USING THE PATTERNS AS TEMPLATES

You can also use the patterns to make templates for cutting and drawing around. Trace the design onto tracing paper then onto thin plastic, for instance the top of a plastic ice cream container. Cut the shape out and you will have a very strong, durable template. Cardboard, oiled parchment and clear acetate are other good materials, which can be used again and again.

USING THE PATTERNS AS STENCILS

A stencil is a very useful way of making a re-usable pattern to

The Grid Method

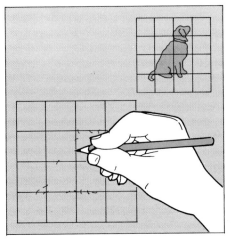 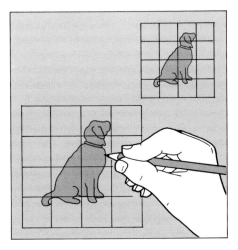 

On a piece of paper, draw up an area of the size you want the finished image to be – larger or smaller depending on whether you want to enlarge or reduce the design. Fill with grid squares matching the pattern of those that surround the original drawing; the important thing is to have the same number of squares on both grid patterns. Now copy the original square by square onto the second version, marking the points at which the original design bisects a line on the new grid.

Follow the points as a guide to where your pen should go. Always check the copied design against the original, and draw over the lines to make sure that they are fluid and continuous.

A variation of this technique is to use it to change the proportions by distorting the original design. For example, to have a design that fits a long, sleek shape, you might decide that the drawing would look best if made thinner. So, draw up a second grid that corresponds in position to the original, but with vertical rectangles instead of squares.

Cutting Stencils

Trace the outline of the selected design onto a sheet of clear acetate or oiled parchment.

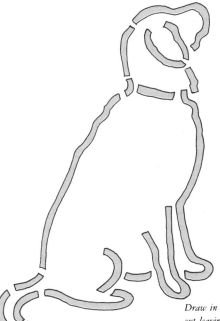

Draw in the internal area to be cut out leaving 'bridges' to hold the stencil together.

repeat shapes onto a variety of surfaces, including paper and card, fabric, ceramics, wood, and sugarpaste- (or fondant-) covered cakes. To make a stencil pattern from the designs in this book, trace the outline onto clear acetate or oiled parchment, and carefully cut it away on the inside using a sharp craft knife. When doing this, remember to build in 'bridges' over the internal lines that divide the main parts of the design, or where you want a change of colour. Beware when cutting a dense or complicated design as much of its main body will be cut away, making it very weak. The bridge-like links should come at regular intervals to hold the stencil together. If you want to avoid using bridges, you will need to cut a separate stencil for each area of colour and apply one after the other, allowing the paint to dry in between.

When cutting your stencil it helps to tape it securely to your cutting surface. Begin with the smaller elements in your design; once the larger ones have been cut out you will lose some of the rigidity of your material and it could rip slightly at the edges. Carefully make firm, smooth cuts towards yourself without using excessive pressure.

When the direction of the cut changes, turn the stencil so that you are still cutting towards yourself, as opposed to turning the knife. Be sure to change your knife blades regularly as they can dull quickly.

A stencil pattern can be used directly onto fabrics (specially designed water-based paints are available, which are 'set' with a hairdryer or by pressing when dry with a hot iron). They are also attractive on walls and make lovely friezes and borders around doorways, ceilings and pictures; a variety of acrylic, emulsion (latex) and oil-based paints are available, and stencil crayons and spray paints can also be used. Wood dyes and stains give a pretty stencilled effect on wooden surfaces, such as small chests or rocking chairs.

When using a stencil, attach it firmly around the edges on the required surface and blot in the colour. Be sure to use edible dusting powders on sugarpaste, but for most decorative purposes you can use standard eggshell or emulsion paint, signwriter's paint, acrylic artist's paint and even car spray paint (which should be applied only in a well-ventilated room).

TRANSFERRING THE PATTERNS ONTO FABRIC

To transfer a design onto fabric for embroidery or painting with fabric paint, first trace the desired drawing on tracing paper to the required size. Place on the fabric and insert pins through the paper around the outline and along the inner line work. Tear the paper away and mark the line of pins with dressmaker's chalk.

Another method is to place a sheet of dressmaker's carbon paper between the traced design and the fabric; go over the pattern again with a sharp instrument or pencil. The carbon lines will transfer to the fabric, and can then be reinforced with dressmaker's chalk or a fabric marking pen. The carbon marks will wash out.

Alternatively, use water-soluble fabric marking pens, tracing the design onto tracing paper and then onto the fabric. If it is thin enough to see through, simply lay the fabric directly over the design and trace. (Place the design under the fabric on a special light box or against a window, and draw directly onto the material.) After the outline has been filled in or embroidered over as required, the pen marks can be washed out in cold water. Fade-out marker pens, too, can be used – the lines do not require washing out but simply fade away. A variety of dressmaker's tracing pencils are also available.

Crewel Work

Once the design has been transferred onto the fabric, lines are then embroidered in to fill in the area. When doing this, draw the lines just as if you were writing with a pen, so that the lines sit evenly and fill in all of the design area.

Appliqué Work

Trace out the component elements of the design and use these to make plastic or cardboard templates. With the templates, cut the shapes out of fabric, paper, or other material, and place them onto the required surface. Once in place, very fine stitches are usually sewn or painted around the edge.

Cut-Out Work

The designs can be adapted for cut-work embroidery, if a simple pattern is chosen. Trace the design onto the fabric, usually firm linen or cotton, cutting out areas as required, but leaving enough 'bridges' so that the holes are not too large or fragile – much the same procedure as cutting out a stencil. The strengthening bars and outlines can be embroidered in a colour to match the fabric.

TRANSFERRING THE PATTERNS ONTO OTHER OBJECTS

Carbon paper can be used to transfer the designs onto 3-dimensional objects, such as pots, ornaments, table-ware, or wood, which can then be painted or drawn over in your chosen style. Trace the design accurately onto a piece of tracing paper cut to a size so that there is a generous margin around the design. Cut a piece of carbon paper to roughly the same size, and position it, carbon-side down, on the area of the object onto which you want to transfer the design. Place the piece of tracing paper on top of the carbon paper, and stick it temporarily in place with a small piece of masking tape (this ensures that the paper does not slip while you are transferring the design). Now draw over the traced lines of the design, pressing hard with the tip of a pencil so that the carbon paper transfers the motif onto the surface. Before removing your design, pull one corner away and check to see that the drawing has transferred completely. If it has not, replace the corner, and you should be able to retrace without creating double lines. By moving it, you can use the same piece of carbon paper many times.

Painting Ceramics

The two most important rules when applying paint with a paint brush are firstly to match the size of the paint brush to the surface you are covering, and secondly not to take up too much paint onto your brush at any one time. Although ceramic paints are quite thick, they can be diluted using water or white spirit (rubbing alcohol); however, if you are using them for the first time, it is worth experimenting first, either on a piece of paper or on a ceramic surface such as a spare tile. Use a thick brush for covering large areas, a fine one for detail work, and try to keep your brush strokes regular, following the same basic direction.

Painting Wood

There are two basic types of paint, water-based and oil-based. Both varieties come in a flat/matt, satin or gloss finish. For painting furniture a flat or matt finish paint is most preferable, as decorative work will adhere better to a duller basecoat. A gloss shine can always be applied after the decoration using a poly-gloss varnish.

Most water-based paints, which can be thinned with water and require only warm, soapy water for cleaning up and washing brushes, are easier to work with than oil-based paints, which render a more brilliant colour and a stronger finish.

With all paints, allow each coat to dry thoroughly before applying successive coats, as the damp layer may wrinkle or bubble under the new layer if it is not allowed full drying time. With oil-based paint, be aware that some contain lead which is toxic if ingested, so you need to be careful when using certain oils on furniture that will be used by children.

TRANSFERRING THE PATTERNS ONTO ICED CAKES

Once you have chosen the design, trace it onto tracing paper and then transfer it onto your royal icing- or fondant-covered cake or plaque surface, making sure the surface is dry and firm. Transferring is best done with a stylus, a metal tool with a minute ball on the end, which is used by placing the pattern onto the required surface and gliding the stylus like a pencil over the design to transfer it. You can then pipe over the embedded outline in icing. A more traditional method is to prick holes through the tracing paper into the surface.

When transferring onto a soft or semi-soft surface, use either a copy projector, which illuminates the design using light reflex onto the cake surface (then pipe or paint directly onto the lines shown), or first pipe the design onto a piece of clear plastic such as perspex or plexiglass, using royal icing made without glycerine. Let this dry and then press the piped design gently but firmly onto the required surface; lift off carefully to reveal an embossed, mirror image outline. Royal icing can be used a few times in this way; if you want to make a permanent embosser, you could pipe the design using a flexible bathroom or kitchen tile sealer rather than icing. This can be used many times.

Using the Patterns for Buttercream and Frosting Work

Trace your required image or combination of designs with a black pen onto tracing paper or cellophane, plexiglass or clear plastic, then, using a copy projector, project the design onto the buttercream-covered cake surface. Pipe over the design with buttercream in a colour of your choice and allow to dry; the inner areas can then be filled with piped buttercream, piping jelly or melted chocolate (candy).

An alternative method is to pipe the design in melted chocolate (candy) onto a piece of glass, perspex or plexiglass, and once set press onto the buttercream-covered cake surface. Pipe over this embossed image with buttercream of a different colour. Remember that by using this method you will get a reverse or mirror image.

Another way is to mark an area onto waxed paper to represent the size of the cake, and pipe the design onto it. Fill in with buttercream, using a different colour for the design in the middle. For example, if your cake is 25cm (10″) you would have a 25cm (10″) circle of buttercream on waxed paper, with the image area of the design filled in the middle. Pipe the buttercream so that it is about 1cm (½″) thick. Then put another piece of waxed paper on top and place in the deep freezer until solid. Pull the top layer off, flip it over onto the cake surface and pull off the bottom layer of waxed paper to reveal the flat, smooth pattern underneath.

Using the Patterns for Sugarcraft Piping

To pipe images in either royal icing or buttercream, trace the basic design onto tracing paper, cut this out and stick it onto the top of a nail or cake pick. Place waxed paper squares over this and pipe on the extra detail or devices. This ensures identical reproduction, with perfect results every time.

Using the Patterns for Sugarcraft Jelly and Wafer Painting

This is a very quick and easy way to place a design onto your cake. Using a piece of rice/wafer paper, trace on the design, using a paint brush and food colouring or melted chocolate (candy), or an edible food colour pen, then stick this face-up directly onto your cake surface. This will be no problem on buttercream, but with sugarpaste (rolled fondant) first lightly steam the surface with a kettle, let it dry a little so that it is just sticky, and then press the design onto the cake surface. Because the rice/wafer paper is absorbed into the cake surface, you will just be left with your chosen design.

HOUSEHOLD PETS

Cats

Cats

Cats

Cats

Dogs

Dogs

Dogs

Dogs

Rabbits

Rabbits

ON THE FARM

Cows

Cows

Horses

Horses

Goats

Sheep

Pigs

Mice

WOODLAND CREATURES

Deer

Squirrels

Foxes

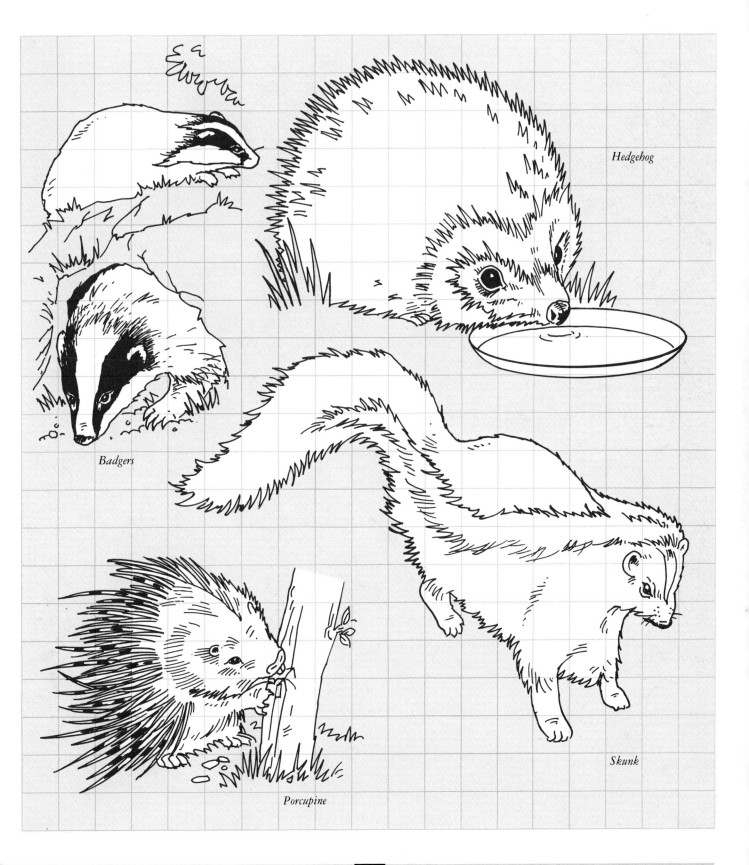

Hedgehog

Badgers

Porcupine

Skunk

IN THE WILD

Rhinoceros

Rhinoceros

Hippopotamus

Elephants

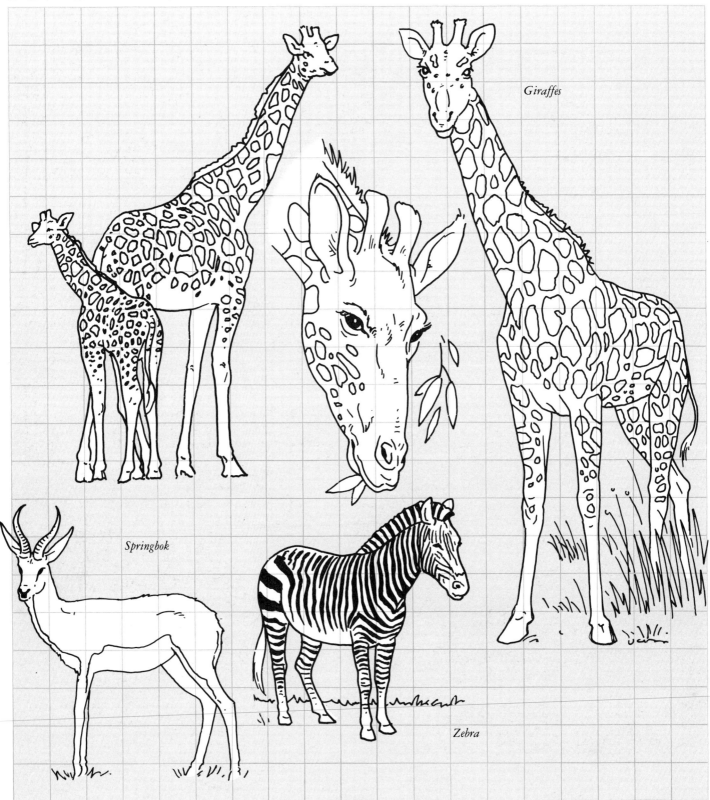

Giraffes

Springbok

Zebra

Apes

Leopard

Lions

Leopard

Tigers

Lion

Lion

Camels

Buffalo & Bison

Polar bears

Bears

Panda

Grizzly bear

Kangaroos

Koalas

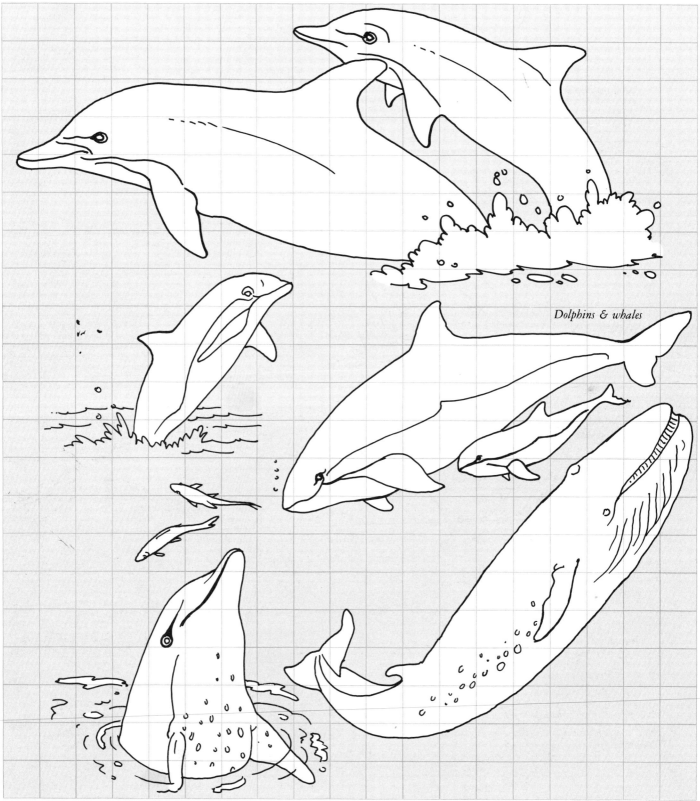

Dolphins & whales

Walrus

Seal

Seal

Sea turtle

Duck-billed platypus

SNAKES AND REPTILES

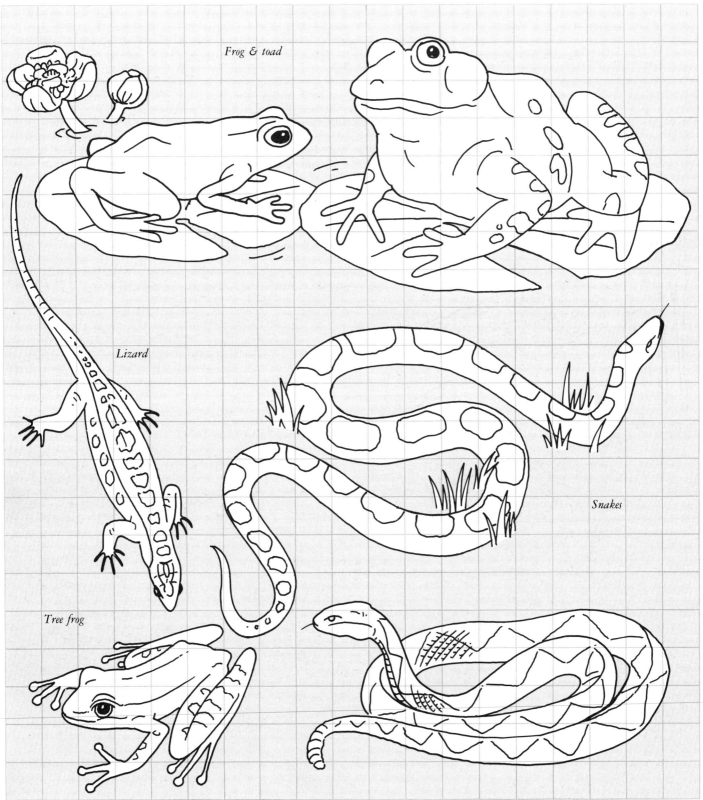

Frog & toad

Lizard

Snakes

Tree frog

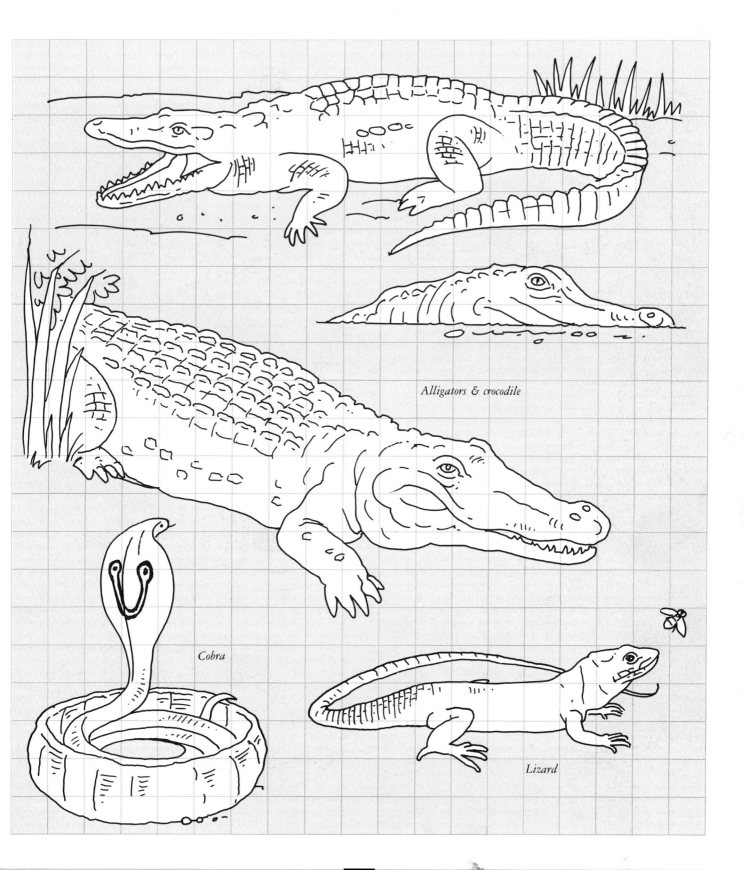

Alligators & crocodile

Cobra

Lizard

BIRDS

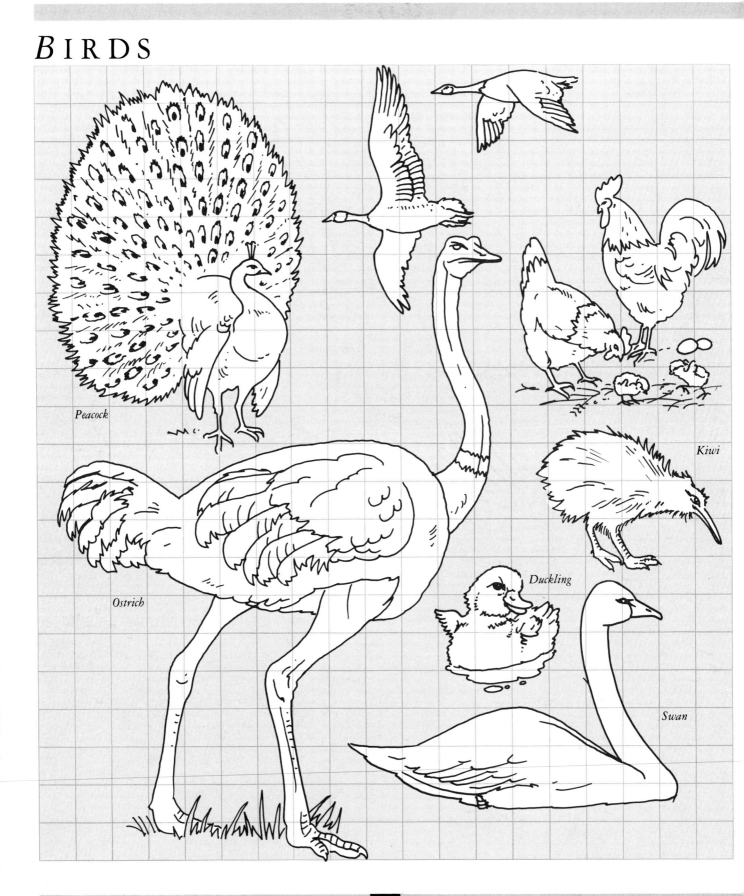

Peacock

Ostrich

Kiwi

Duckling

Swan

Pelican

Penguins

Eagle

Ducks

BIRDS

Pelican

Goose

Owls